CROSSWORDS

FOR

KIDS

by
Dr. Linda Lawrence

Illustrated by
Tracey Downs

Edited by
Mike Reardon

ISBN 0-9716039-0-1

BE AN EXPERT!

Answers to puzzles are found at the back of the book. The page number of the puzzle is the puzzle number for the answers.

IT IS

NOT

CHEATING

TO USE THE

ANSWERS!

Just try to do the puzzle by yourself first. Then use the answers to help you finish. You will automatically learn new words each time and then you'll be an

expert!

YOU CAN DO IT!

1. BE SURE YOU KNOW THE WORDS IN THE WORD LIST.

2. THINK ABOUT WHAT DIFFERENT MEANINGS THE WORDS AND CLUES MIGHT HAVE.

3. FILL IN ALL THE **ACROSS** WORDS THAT YOU KNOW FOR SURE. BE SURE TO USE A PENCIL, NOT INK.

4. FILL IN ALL THE **DOWN** WORDS THAT YOU KNOW.

5. NOW GO BACK AND FILL IN ANY NEW **ACROSS** WORDS THAT YOU CAN FIGURE OUT.

6. DO THE SAME WITH ANY NEW **DOWN** WORDS YOU CAN FIGURE OUT.

7. NOW SKIP AROUND AND TRY TO FILL IN THE REST OF THE WORDS.

8. IF YOU GET STUCK, LOOK UP ONE OR TWO WORDS IN THE ANSWERS FOR SOME HELP, OR LOOK IN THE WORD LIST.

TRICKS

Many words have different meanings (called synonyms) and the puzzles have clues based on these tricky meanings. Look at the words below and write sentences for all the different meanings you can think of beside them. You can write them on the lines on the following page.

EXAMPLE: FLY
     1. The fly crawled on the wall.
     2. The boy caught a fly ball.
     3. Did your mom fly to New York?

Here are your words to try:
    1. show
    2. sign
    3. bend
    4. ship
    5. square

SPECIAL ENDINGS

If you don't know a word, but know it ends in a special ending, write the ending letters in the boxes FIRST and they may help you figure out other words. Here are some endings that are used:

pre	Means before
i.e.	Abbreviation that means FOR EXAMPLE
prefix	Letters at the beginning of a word to change the meaning
suffix	Letters at the end of a word to change the meaning
S (and ES)	Letters at the end of a word to indicate more than one
est	Letters at the end of a word that mean the MOST or BEST
re	Letters in front of a word meaning to do over again
er	Letters at the end meaning MORE

SPECIAL HINTS

ET	**LATIN WORD FOR "AND"**
ET CETERA	**TWO LATIN WORDS MEANING "AND SO FORTH"**
C.E.	**COMMON ERA (means the same as B.C.)**
B.C.E.	**BEFORE THE COMMON ERA (same as B.C.)**

Games with words are often used. "Middle of the Boat" can be "OA". Or "King beater (Ace) Get it?

Foreign words are used such as "tia."
(Spanish for "aunt")
and "ein" (German for one)

Sometimes part of a word or phrase is used:
_ _ _ *la-la* The answer is T R A
(The three blanks means that there are three letters in the answer.)
Wizard of _ _   The answer is OZ
(You'll have fun figuring them out!)

ROMAN NUMERALS

The ancient Romans invented a clever way to write numbers. It was so clever that we still use it today on watches, outlines, book chapters and lots of other things. What they did was use capital letters to stand for the important numbers like 5, 10, 50, 100, and 1000 and so forth.

5 was written as V

and

10 was written as X

Then they put I's before (if subtracting) or after (if adding) the letters to show how many ONES you add or subtract from the letter.

EXAMPLE:

To write 5, they wrote V

To write 4 they put a I
        before the V (4 = 5 - 1)
            So 4 = IV

To write 6, they added a I
        after the V (6 = 5 + 1)
            So 6 = VI

To write 10, they wrote X
        So 15 = XV
                (15 = 10 + 5)

1	I
2	II
3	III
4	IV
5	V
6	VI
7	VII
8	VIII
9	IX
10	X
11	XI
12	XII
13	XIII
14	XIV
15	XV
16	XVI
17	XVII
18	XVIII
19	XIX
20	XX
21	XXI
22	XXII
24	XXIV
25	XXV
26	XXVI
30	XXX
31	XXXI
40	XL
41	XLI
49	IL
50	L
100	C
500	C
1000	M

HAPPY

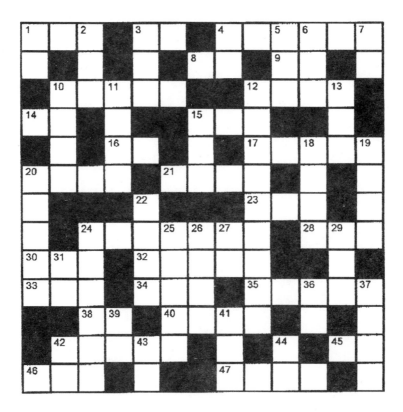

ACROSS

1. Plaything
3. Mister in Mexico and Spain: abbrev.
4. Polite form of address
8. Leaf of a tea plant
9. See 7 DOWN
10. Elated
12. Three feet
14. Common Era (also A.D.)
15. Expert
16. Part of the personality
17. Old fashioned blackboard
20. Reach
21. Opposite of east
23. Age, period of time

24. Less expensive
28. One of the Three Stooges
30. Spanish for gold
32. Kind of antelope
33. What you do with oars
34. Short for UNTIL
35. Old saying
38. Little _ _ Beep
40. So; ultra
42. Animal used for work and pleasure
45. Do, Re, _ _
46. Opposite of GIRL
47. Float gently in the air

DOWN

1. Toward
2. Old word for YES
3. Eat, dine; from the word for SUPPER
4. Do, Re, _ _
5. Señora: abbrev.
6. Black goo for sealing things
7. Egyptian god
10. Aid
11. Ache
12. Day before today
13. A small spot; a period
15. See 15 ACROSS
18. First man in the Bible
19. Make easier; loosen; rest
20. Mister in Mexico and Spain
22. Encounter
24. One who works with cattle
25. Having life
26. Without much color; dim
27. Spanish for IN
29. Organization: abbrev.; part of a web address
31. Or backwards
36. Is; part of TO BE
37. Send; spew forth
39. Partner of EITHER
41. Uncooked
42. Part of what Santa says
43. Very
44. Coming from

ACE	OF	
ADAGE	OR	
ADAM	ORG	
ALIVE	ORO	
AR	PAIN	
BO	PALE	
BOY	RA	
CE	RAW	
CHEAPER	ROW	
COWBOY	SEÑOR	
DOT	SLATE	
EASE	SO	
ELAND	SPAN	
EMIT	SR	
EN	SR	
ERA	SRA	
HAPPY	SUP	
HELP	TAR	
HO	TI	
HORSE	TIL	
ID	TO	
MEET	TOY	
MI	VERY	
MOE	WAFT	
	WEST	
	YARD	
	YEA	
	YESTERDAY	

EON

ACROSS

1. Me
6. Not even
8. Two vowels
9. Plaything
11. Trousers
13. Uncooked
14. Sound of surprises
15. Cut-off trousers
17. Ancient Egyptian god
19. Age, period of time
20. A girl's name
21. Inanimate object
22. Doctor: abbrev.
23. A lower singing voice
28. Precious metal
30. Expert
32. Station: abbrev.
33. Not YES
35. Language spoken in Mexico
38. Sew
39. Exist
40. Liquid used for writing
42. Climbing _ _ the ladder
43. Opposite of RICH
45. Short for FATHER
46. Opposite of FROM
48. Ratio between diameter and circumference
49. Letter before "S"
50. Exists
51. You need it to buy anything

DOWN

2. A YES vote
3. Partner of OR
4. _ _ _ Vegas
5. Very
6. Not others
7. Below
10. Three feet
11. They settled in New England
12. Negative
15. Unhappy
16. A bluish-green color
18. Toward
24. YOU in Spanish
25. Partner of EITHER
26. Myself
27. Twenty in Rome
28. Smelled
29. Motel
31. Small bed
32. Spanish: abbrev.
34. Heavenly body
35. Floating vesssels
36. Same as 50 ACROSS
37. Elated
41. Not Applicable: abbrev.
43. Same as 45 ACROSS
44. Partner of EITHER
46. Opposite of FROM
47. Opposite of OFF

ACE
ALTO
AM
AR
AT
COT
DEE
DOWN
DR
EITHER
ERA
HAPPY
IA
INK
INN
IS
IT
LAS
ME
MONEY
MYSELF
NA
NO
ODD
OH
ON
OR
OURSELVES
PA
PANTS
PI

POOR
PURITANS
RA
RAW
SAD
SHIPS
SHORTS
SILVER
SO
SP
SPANISH
STALK
STAR
STITCH
STN
TE
TEAL
TO
TOY
UP
XX
YARD
YEA

SLO - MO

ACROSS

2. Part of the foot
5. Hourglass filler
7. Same as 1 DOWN
8. Slang for "What?"
9. Poisonous snake
10. Mourn
12. Expert
14. Toward
16. Years after Christ
17. Inside
18. Battery size
20. 5,280 feet
21. Sew
22. Funny!

23. Come nearer
27. Unhappy
29. Letter before S (phonetically)
31. Concealed
32. Short for NORMAN
33. _ _ _ mo (in TV and movie filming)
34. Fifteen in Rome
35. Very
36. Me
40. Male turkey
41. Mister in Mexico and Spain: abbrev.
43. Part of good-bye in London
45. Very
46. A kind of ship

DOWN

1. A doctor's degree
2. Saying
3. Male sheep
4. Less expensive
5. Language spoken in Mexico
6. Doctor: abbrev.
7. Polite form of address for a woman
9. Same as 14 ACROSS
11. North Dakota: abbrev.
13. Per
15. Short for until
17. Neutral object pronoun
19. Sound of surprise
21. Mrs. in Mexico and Spain: abbrev.
23. Put together
24. Trousers
25. Tool for rowing
26. Colorado: abbrev.
27. Floating vessels
28. First two letters of AID
29. In addition; too
30. Part of a house
37. Positive answer
38. Latin for AND
39. _ _ _ Vegas
40. A kind of hat
42. Egyptian god
44. Myself

AA
ACE
AD
ADAGE
ADD
AHA
AI
ALSO
AM
APPROACH
AR
ARCH
ASP
AT
CHEAPER
CO
DAH
DR
EACH
ET
HA
HID
IN
IT
LAMENT
LAS
MAAM
MD
ME

MILE
MYSELF
ND
NORM
NORTH
OAR
PANTS
RA
RAM
ROOM
SAD
SAND
SHIPS
SLO
SO
SPANISH
SR
SRA
STEAMER
STITICH
TA
TAM
TIL
TOM
XV
YEA

PURITANS

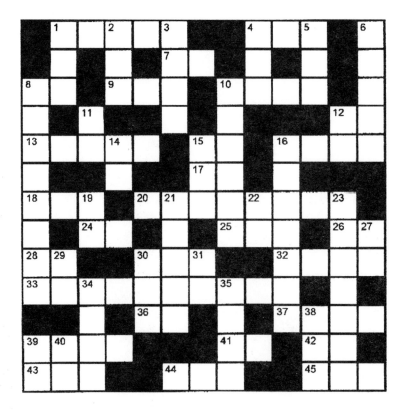

ACROSS

1. Old fashioned blackboard
4. Not even
7. Six in Rome
8. Above
9. Girl's name
10. Twelve inches
12. Nickname for Alfred
13. Staff of life
15. Opposite of NOR
16. Precious metal
17. First two letters of the alphabet
18. Age, period of time
20. They settled in New England
24. Myself

25. Prefix meaning to undo
26. River in Europe
28. THE in Spanish
30. Point
32. Reach
33. Help
36. Physical Education: abbrev.
37. Floating vessel
39. Opposite of RICH
41. Negative word
42. Exists
43. Poisonous snake
44. Yes to a sailor
45. Be quiet!

DOWN

1. Eat, dine; short for supper
2. Put together
3. Opposite of ODD
4. Spanish for gold
5. A small point of ink
6. Construct
8. Used to shield the sun
10. Prohibit
11. Myself, I
12. Nickname for Albert
14. Letter before S
15. Tool for rowing
16. Vessels for holding liquid
19. Exist
21. Bring together
22. Leaf of a tea plant
23. Language spoken in Mexico
27. Opposite of OFF
29. _ _ I was saying
30. Same as 43 ACROSS
31. Short for MOTHER
34. Halt
35. Name of Columbus' ship
38. Belonging to him
39. Short for Papa
40. Operating System: abbrev.

AB	
ADD	
AIM	ODD
AL	ON
AM	OR
AR	ORO
AS	OS
ASP	PA
ASSISTANCE	PE
BREAD	PO
BUILD	POOR
DEE	PURITANS
DIS	SHH
DOT	SHIP
ERA	SLATE
EVEN	SPAN
FOOT	SPANISH
FORBID	STOP
GLASSES	SUP
GOLD	TI
HIS	UMBRELLA
IS	UNITE
LA	UP
MA	UP
ME	VI
NINA	VI
NO	YEA
OAR	

JAPANESE KIMONO

ACROSS

1. Cut-off trousers
6. One who jumps across
10. Funny!
11. Part of good-bye in London
13. Toward
14. See 28 ACROSS
15. Not a soprano
18. List of bequests
19. Egyptian god
20. Short for MOTHER
21. Japanese robe
25. Per
27. Scare sound
28. Part of the personality
29. Send

31. Grate
34. That hurts!
36. _ _ _ la la
37. Come nearer
40. Doctor: abbrev.
42. Slippery, long fish
43. Greek "R"
44. Old fashioned blackboard
47. Forbid
49. Tool for weaving
50. Operating system
52. Half a laugh
53. Go fast
54. Lid

DOWN

1. Floating vessel
2. Possessed
3. Sound of surprise
4. Ancient Egyptian god
5. Stem
7. Word used to compare
8. AND in Rome
9. Computer term
12. Nickname for Alonzo
16. Burial site
17. Spanish for gold
18. Women's branch of the armed forces
20. Angry
22. Sound of pleasure
23. Top of a map
24. Eat, dine
25. Partner of OR
26. Aid
30. Also
32. Letter after "Q"
33. Unhappy
35. Armed conflict between countries
37. In addition
38. Baby buggy in England
39. Spoil
41. Uncooked
45. Land to build a house on
46. Age; period of time
47. Before the common era
48. Negative word
49. THE in Spanish
51. Very

AL	NOT
ALSO	OH
ALTO	OO
APPROACH	ORO
AR	OS
AS	OW
BAN	PRAM
BCE	RA
BOO	RACE
DR	RASP
EACH	RAW
EEL	RO
EITHER	ROM
EMIT	ROT
ERA	SAD
ET	SHIP
HA	SHORTS
HAD	SLATE
HAHA	SO
HELP	STALK
ID	SUP
KIMONO	TA
LA	TOMB
LEAPER	TO
LOOM	TOO
LOT	TOP
MA	TOR
MAD	TRA
NORTH	WAC
	WAR
	WILL

ADAGE

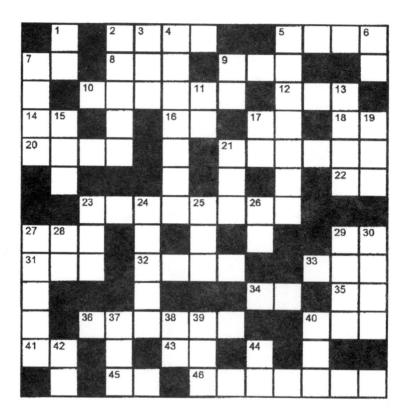

ACROSS

2. Part of a foot
5. Hourglass filler
7. Myself
8. Slang for "What?"
9. Poisonous snake
10. Mourn
12. Expert
14. Toward
16. Years after Christ
17. Inside
18. Battery size
20. 5,280 feet
21. Sew
22. Funny!

23. Come nearer
27. Unhappy
29. Letter before S (phonetically)
31. Concealed
32. Short for NORMAN
33. _ _ _ mo (in TV)
34. Fifteen in Rome
35. Very
36. Me
40. Male turkey
41. Mister in Mexico and Spain: abbrev.
43. Part of good-bye in London
45. Exist
46. Old kind of ship

DOWN

1. Myself
2. Saying
3. Male sheep
4. Less expensive
5. Language spoken in Mexico
6. Doctor: abbrev.
7. Polite form of address to a woman
9. Same as 14 ACROSS
11. North Dakota: abbrev.
13. Per
15. Short for until
17. Neutral object
19. Sound of surprise
21. Mrs. in Mexico and Spain: abbrev.
23. Put together
24. Trousers
25. Tool for rowing
26. Colorado: abbrev.
27. Floating vessels
28. First two letters of AID
29. In addition
30. Part of a house
37. Old-fashioned YES
38. Latin for AND
39. _ _ _ Vegas
40. A kind of hat
42. Egyptian god
44. Myself

AA	MILE
ACE	MYSELF
AD	ND
ADAGE	NORM
ADD	NORTH
AHA	OAR
AI	PANTS
ALSO	RA
AM	RAM
APPROACH	ROOM
AR	SAD
ARCH	SAND
ASP	SHIPS
AT	SLO
CHEAPER	SO
CO	SPANISH
DAH	SR
DR	SRA
EACH	STEAMER
ET	STITCH
HA	TA
HID	TAM
IN	TIL
LAMENT	TOM
LAS	XV
MAAM	YEA
MD	
ME	

FOOD

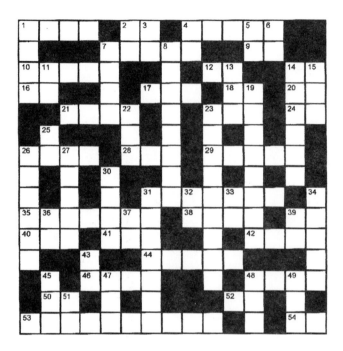

ACROSS

1. Energy for humans
2. Abbreviation for MASTER
   OF CEREMONIES
4. A is for ----
7. Juicy fruit with a fuzzy skin
9. Toward
10. Soupy gravy-like food
12. Beast of burden
14. Abbreviation for CALIFORNIA
16. "Abbreviation for HEIGHT
17. Abbreviation for INTENSIVE
   CARE UNIT
18. Fifteen in Rome
20. From
21. Meat of pigs
23. SEVEN in Rome
26. A few

28. Corn on the ----
29. Fruit from which wine is made
31. Necessary food group
35. A green fruit
38. Water that comes from the sky
39. Myself
40. An evil deed
41. A small child
42. Soft drink
44. Same as 4 ACROSS
46. The most common spice
48. Bones around the chest
50. Abbreviation for EACH
52. YES in Spanish
53. Large, juicy fruit that's red inside
54. Abbreviation for QUART

DOWN

1. Creatures that live in water
2. Myself
3. Same as 14 ACROSS
4. Open wide and say ____!
5. Tra-La—
6. AND in Rome
7. A partridge in a ---- tree
8. Fruit from which pickles
        are made
11. Toward
13. TWENTY-ONE in Rome
14. Beverage made from ground
       beans
15. Rear of a boat
19. Vegetables are full of them
22. Where to go for fried chicken
23. Edible plant
25. Toward
26. Zucchini is one
27. Cantaloup is one
30. Not hilly
31. Wrong way to spell POTATO
32. Partner of EITHER
33. After C (from a spelling rule)
34. They're high in protein
36. SIX in Rome
37. Act
39. Initials after a Medical
      Doctor's name
43. Exists
45. Opposite of ISN'T
47. It's what we breath
48. A bone around the chest
49. Cooked over coals or a fire
51. Toward

AVOCADO	OF	
APPLE	OR	
AFT	OX	
AH	PEACH	
AIR	PEAR	
AT	PORK	
BBQ	POTATO	
BEANS	PROTEIN	
CA	QT	
COB	RAIN	
COFFEE	RIB	
CUCUMBER	RIBS	
DO	SALT	
EA	SAUCE	
EI	SI	
ET	SIN	
FISH	SODA	
FOOD	SOME	
FT	SQUASH	
GRAPE	TEA	
HT	TO	
ICU	TOT	
IS	VI	
KFC	VII	
LA	VEGETABLE	
MC	VITAMINS	
MD	WATERMELON	
ME	XV	
MEAT	XXI	
MELON		

NEW MEXICO

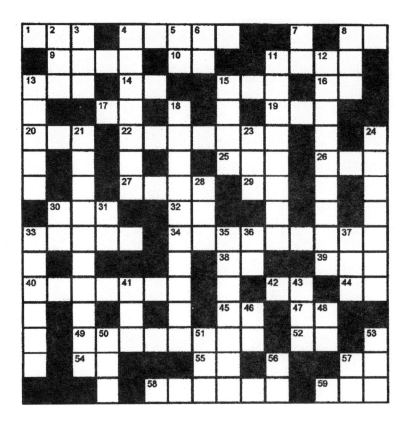

ACROSS

1. A way to send a package
4. A northeastern state
8. Exist
9. A mid-western state
10. Opposite of FROM
11. Opposite of UP
13. Exist
14. Negative
15. Indian tribe
16. Part of the personality
17. Toward
19. _ _ _ Vegas
20. Muscle spasm usually in the eye
22. A Southern state
25. Question about way of doing
26. Needed to row a boat
27. Oohhs and _____
29. Washington: abbrev.

30. Three in Rome
32. Except after C
33. Slang for REALLY GOOD
34. Its capitol is Santa Fe
38. Old word for YOU
39. Nickname for Nancy
40. State in the Northeast where maple
        syrup comes from
42. Four in Rome
44. Not Applicable: abbrev.
45. Do, Re, _ _
47. Exists
49. Lincoln was from this state
52. Part of the personality
54. Exist
55. A nurse's degree
57. First two vowels
58. State south of Washington
59. South by southeast

DOWN

2. Beginning of portly
3. Opposite of HE
4. Northeast ranching state
5. Inanimate object
6. Negative
7. Very
8. Also
11. Washington crossed it
12. The Dairy State
13. Religious table
15. State settled by Brigham Young
18. Farthest state to the northwest
21. State where gold was discovered
23. Cut the grass
24. The Grand Canyon State
28. Look
30. Two in Rome
31. Same as 5 DOWN
33. Las Vegas is there
35. Its capitol is Cheyenne
36. Myself
37. Is able
41. Gasoline is made from it
43. Seven in Rome
46. Exists
48. South Dakota: abbrev.
50. H,I,J,K,_,_,_
51. What a miner looks for
53. Look
56. Opposite of OFF
57. A comparative word; Easy _ _ pie.

AE
AHHS
ALABAMA
ALTAR
AND
AM
ARE
ARIZONA
AS
CALIFORNIA
CAN
DELAWARE
DOWN
HOW
ID
IE
II
III
ILLINOIS
IS
IT
IV
LAS
LMN
MAINE
MONTANA
MOW
ME

MI
NA
NAN
NEVADA
NEW MEXICO
NIFTY
NO
OAR
OHIO
OIL
ON
ORE
OREGON
POR
RN
SD
SEE
SHE
SO
SSE
TIC
TO
UPS
UTAH
UTE
VERMONT
VII
WA
WASHINGTON
WISCONSIN
WYOMING
YE

BLUSH

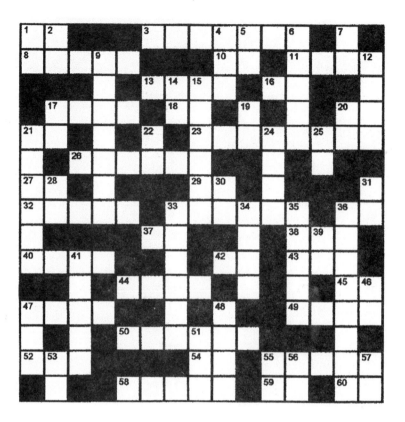

ACROSS

1. Opposite of DOWN
3. Worn on the nose to aid the eyes
8. Clothing with legs
10. Take to much
11. It grows on your head
13. The edges of a mouth
16. Short for HELLO
17. It's at the end of your arm
18. Very
20. Air Conditioning: initials
21. Ancient Egyptian god
23. Color for lips
26. Small 2-piece bathing suit
27. Exist
29. Same as 18 ACROSS
32. Turn red with embarrassment
33. Short pants
36. Exist

37. Sound of surprise
38. Auto
40. Organ for smell
42. Attached to
43. American Medical Association
44. Old-fashioned long blouse
45. California: abbrev.
47. On the end of the fingers and toes
49. We walk on them
50. Fine dust
52. Covering for the head
54. Middle of BOAT
55. Coverings for the feet
58. Dark pencil for highlighting the eyelashes
59. Male pronoun
60. Opposite of FROM

DOWN

1. Same as 1 ACROSS
2. Father
4. Help!
5. South Dakota: abbrev.
6. Clothing worn on the upper body
7. Spanish for YES
9. Slang for tennis shoes
12. Short for Richard
14. Exist
15. Shine
17. Half a laugh
19. Opposite of DOWN
20. Same as 20 ACROSS
21. Bright cloth tied in hair
22. Same as 7 DOWN
24. Matching set of clothes
25. Exist
28. Room addition
30. Sound of surprise
31. Fifth letter (phonetically)
33. Follow; image made in the shade
34. Skin on fruit
35. Cloth to tie around the head or neck
36. Jewelry worn on the wrist
39. Exist
41. Clothing worn by girls
46. Toward
47. Slang for NO
48. Listen
51. Female deer
53. Alcoholics anonymous: abbrev.
55. Quiet!
56. Opposite of SHE
57. Very

AA	NOSE
AC	OA
AM	OD
AMA	ON
AT	OO
BE	PA
BIKINI	PANTS
BLUSH	POLISH
BRACELET	POWDER
CA	RA
CAR	RIBBON
DOE	RICK
EE	RING
EH	SCARF
EL	SD
FEET	SH
GLASSES	SHADOW
HA	SHIRT
HAIR	SHOES
HAND	SHORTS
HAT	SKIRT
HE	SI
HEAR	SO
HI	SOS
IS	SUIT
LINER	TENNIES
LIPS	TO
LIPSTICK	UP
MIDI	
NAH	
NAIL	

RASP

ACROSS

1. Aid
5. All Terrain Vehicle
7. Goody!
8. Small bed
10. Actual
11. Middle of the BOOK
12. Not cooked
14. Part of the mind
16. Negative
18. Kind of file; to grind against
20. A ONE in a deck of cards
21. Us
24. Prefix meaning CLOSED IN
25. Cut a little piece
27. Wave back and forth
28. Above

30. Opposite of woman
31. Halt
32. Opposite of SHE
36. AND in Rome
37. ONE in Germany
39. Govern
41. AND in Latin
43. Abbreviation for ROUTE
44. Connecting Romeo with Juliette
46. After the birth of Christ
47. Prefix for COPTER
49. 1,3,5,7...
51. Psst!
52. Definite article
53. What you do with a book

DOWN

1. Four -legged animal
2. Half of a volcano
3. They arrest criminals
4. Act
5. Dam over the Nile in Egypt
6. Six in Rome
8. Prefix meaning Against
9. Abbreviation for TRAIL
13. Letter before S
15. Infer
17. Possess
19. About 3.14
22. Opposite of neither
23. Is able
26. Forbid
29. Short message
33. Partner of OR
34. Build
35. List of candidates
38. Construct
40. Prefix meaning IN
42. A little bit
45. Accomplish
48. Organ for seeing
50. Same as 45 DOWN

AD
ACE
AND
AR
ATV
ASWAN
BAN
BUILD
CAN
CON
COT
DENOTE
DO
EN
EIN
EITHER
ERECT
ET
EYE
FA
FAN
HE
HELI
HELP
HEY
HORSE
ID
LOA
MAN

NO
NOTE
ODD
ON
OO
OWN
PI
POLICE
RASP
RAW
READ
REAL
RT
RULE
SLATE
SNIP
STOP
TAD
THE
TR
VI
WE

STATES

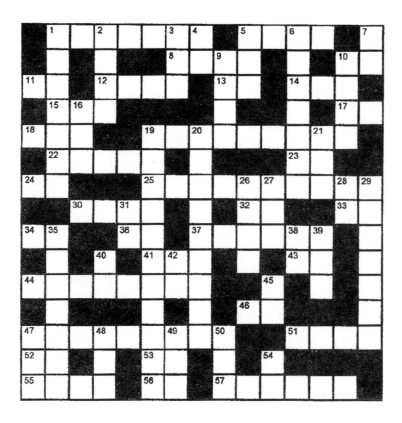

ACROSS

1. Phoenix is the capitol
5. Pulls along by a chain or rope
8. Individual
10. Partner of EITHER
11. GO in Spanish and abbreviation for Virginia
12. Opposite of EAST
13. First two vowels
14. Exclamation of surprise
15. Sheep sound
17. Exists
18. Automobile club
19. Santa Fe is the capitol
22. New England state
23. Opposite of YES
24. South America: abbrev.
25. Our first president
30. State north of Arizona and east of Nevada

32. Opposite of FROM
33. Northeast: abbrev.
34. Four in Rome
36. Nickname for MOTHER
37. State south of Washington
41. Opposite of WOMAN
43. Exist
44. President Clinton's state
46. Medical doctor
47. Baton Rouge is there
51. To lie in warmth
52. Indefinite article
53. Railroad: abbrev.
55. Stalk of a flower
56. Fifth letter
57. Lots of corn grows here

DOWN

1. A southern state
2. A Midwestern state that grows corn
3. Web-like structure
4. Alcoholics Anonymous: abbrev
5. YOU in prayers
6. State where Grand Teton Mountains
     are located
7. Master: abbrev.
9. Peaceful
10. Cleveland is there
16. American Automobile Association:
     initials
19. New England state with two words
20. The Dairy State
21. Small bed
26. Single object
27. Drink originally made with rum
28. Attached
29. Where United Nations building is
31. Hours before noon
35. State famous for maple syrup
38. Doctor who delivers babies
39. Nevada: abbrev.
40. Los Angeles: abbrev.
42. Same as 4 DOWN
45. Years after Christ's birth; also CE
47. _ _ _ Vegas
48. Suffix meaning a belief
49. Exist
50. Question
54. Same as 28 DOWN

AA	
AAA	MAN
AD	MD
AE	MR
ALABAMA	NE
AM	NET
AN	NEW HAMPSHIRE
ARE	NEV
ARIZONA	NEW MEXICO
ARKANSAS	NEW YORK
ASK	NO
BAA	NOG
BASK	OB
BE	OHIO
CALM	OOH
COT	ON
EACH	OR
EE	OREGON
IOWA	RR
IS	SA
ISM	STEM
ITEM	THE
IV	TO
KANSAS	TOWS
LA	UTAH
LAS	VA
LOUISIANA	VERMONT
MA	WASHINGTON
MAINE	WEST
	WISCONSIN
	WYOMING

AMITY

ACROSS

2. 5,280 feet
5. Friendship
9. Toward
10. Aches
11. National Basketball Association
14. Greek letter
15. Street: abbrev.
17. Japanese robe
20. Opposite of FROM
21. Bring together
22. Middle of WAIL
23. General Electric: abbrev.
24. Partner of EITHER
25. Grate
27. See 15 ACROSS
29. Reach
30. Department of Public Safety
31. Make easier, loosen
33. Middle of BOAT
34. Station: abbrev.
35. "This _ _ House"
36. Words set to music
38. Partner of EITHER
39. Age, period of time
42. Organ for hearing
44. Use eyes
46. Doctor: abbrev.
48. See 35 ACROSS
49. Language spoken in Mexico
51. Letter before S, phonetically
53. Opposite of OFF
54. Twenty in Rome
55. Spanish for gold

DOWN

1. Light red
2. Polite form of address
3. Neuter object
4. AND in Rome
5. Battery size
6. Polite form of address
7. Opposite of OUT OF
8. Backwards street abbreviation
10. They settled in New England
12. Mark left by teeth
13. Opposite of OFF
16. Floating vessels
18. Sound of surprise
19. Not others
22. Poisonous snake
23. Vessels for holding liquid
26. Saying
27. Mrs. in Mexico and Spain
28. Part of good-byes in England
32. Very
33. See 13 DOWN
37. Not even
40. OR backwards
41. Not a soprano
43. Application: abbrev.
44. Evil action
45. "What?" in Canada
47. Egyptian god
50. Negative word
52. Same as 40 DOWN

AA	ON
ADAGE	OR
AI	ORO
ALTO	OURSELVES
AMITY	PAINS
APP	PINK
AR	PURITANS
ASP	RA
AT	RASP
BITE	RO
DPS	SEE
DR	SEÑORA
EAR	SHIPS
EASE	SIN
EH	SO
ERA	SONG
ET	SPAN
GE	SPANISH
GLASSES	ST
INTO	STN
IT	TA
KIMONO	TO
MAAM	TS
MILE	UNITE
MISTER	XX
MU	
NBA	
NO	
OA	
ODD	
OH	
OL	

AUSTRALIA

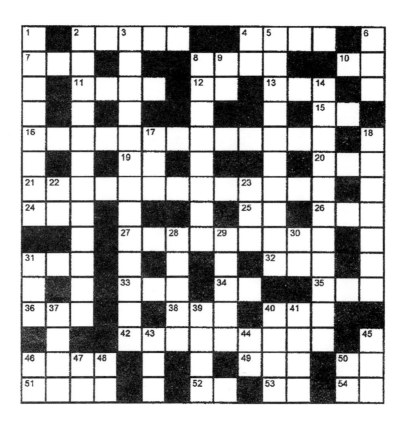

ACROSS

2. A little bit fat
4. Worse than not nice
7. Dessert with a crust
8. Plant with lacy leaves
10. Opposite of FROM
11. Small boat
12. Sound of hesitation
13. Gave food to
15. AND in Rome
16. Chances to do something
19. Same as 10 ACROSS
20. Snoop
21. Distance around the edge of a circle
24. A long laugh
25. Road: abbrev.
26. Spoil
27. The smallest continent

31. Glide down a snowy hill
32. Rhymes with SET
33. Organ for seeing
34. Maybe; on condition
35. Old fashioned man's name
36. Opposite of woman
38. Prefix meaning badly or a mistake
40. Everyone
42. Not today or tomorrow
46. Who _ _ _ _ the door?
49. Tool for rowing
50. Do, Re, _ _
51. Burial place
52. Myself
53. Degree a doctor has
54. Part of the personality

DOWN

1. Come close
2. Result of physical exercise
3. Too bad
4. Railroad: abbrev.
5. Not nice
6. CD _ _ _
8. The most entertaining
9. Nickname for Emily in THE
   WIZARD OF OZ
14. Frantically
17. Male turkey
18. Suspenseful story
22. Middle of DIAL
23. Period of history
28. Stalks
29. Lift
30. Except after C (Part of a
   Spelling clue)
31. Total
37. Too
39. Thing on a list
40. First man in the Bible
41. Shortening made from animal fat
43. Organ for seeing
44. Beginning of Robert
45. Acted
46. Thing
47. Exist
48. Tuberculosis: abbrev.
50. Third note of musical scale

ADAM
ALL
ALSO
AM
APPROACH
AUSTRALIA
CIRCUMFER-
   ENCE
DESPERATELY
DID
ELY
EM
ERA
ET
EYE
FED
FERN
FUNNIEST
HAA
IA
ID
IE
IF
IS AT
IT
ITEM
LARD
MAN
MD
ME
MI
MIS

MYSTERY
OPPORTUNITIES
OAR
PERSPIRATION
PIE
PLUMP
PRY
RAFT
RAISE
RD
RO
ROM
ROT
RR
RUDE
RUSE
SKI
STEMS
SUM
TB
TO
TOM
TOMB
UM
UNFORTU-
   NATELY
UNFRIENDLY
YESTERDAY
YET

MOUNTAINTOP

ACROSS

1. High areas on the earth
8. Most common article
9. Letter before T
11. Incline the head
12. Opposite of OUT
14. Daily publication
17. Organ for hearing
18. Female sheep
19. Kind of whale
20. Went very fast
21. Toward
22. Given as an honor

24. Like
25. Same as 12 ACROSS
26. System for the hearing impaired
27. Same as 20 ACROSS
29. California: abbrev
31. Full of daring
36. Quiet!
38. China is on this continent
40. Opposite of SIT
42. Injure
43. Partner of EITHER

DOWN

1. Way of doing; style
2. Knows the meaning of
3. Less fat
4. An object
5. New Hampshire: abbrev
6. Degrees of heat
7. At a right angle to another
10. Thin threads
13. Northeast: abbrev
15. Adult female
16. Prize
23. Partner of EITHER
25. Lodge
28. Alcoholics Anonymous: abbrev.
30. Like
32. Kind of curve
33. Drink brewed from leaves
34. Remains of a fire
35. Noise and confusion
37. Part of a laugh
38. Exist
39. Maybe
41. Opposite of FROM

AA
ADO
ADVENTUROUS
AM
AS
ASH
ASIA
AT
AWARD
AWARDED
CA
EAR
ESS
EWE
HA
HARM
IF
IN
INN
IT
MANNER
NE
NEWSPAPER
MOUNTAINTOP
NH
NOD
OR
PERPENDICULAR
RAN
SH
SPERM
STAND
STRANDS
TDI
TEA
TEMPERATURES
THE
THINNER
TO
UNDERSTANDS
WOMAN

BITS AND PIECES

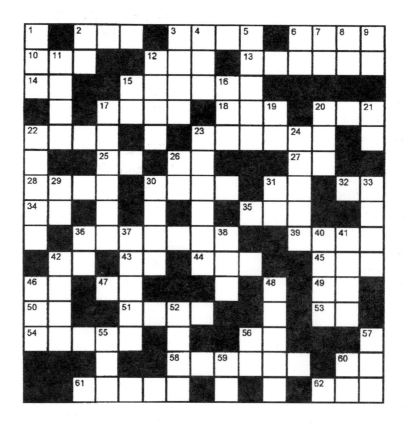

ACROSS

2. Also
3. Insect
6. Chances
10. Everyone
12. Short for until
13. The rest
14. Eleven in Rome
15. Made of Gold
17. Earth
18. King in Rome; common name for a dog
20. In addition
22. Finest
23. Adage; ex: "The early bird gets the worm."
25. Thing
26. YES in Mexico and Spain
27. Fifth letter of the alphabet
28. Give off
30. Precious metal
31. Four in Rome
32. Abbreviation for AIR CONDITIONING

34. First two vowels
35. Tell an untruth
36. Less expensive
39. Reign
42. Abbreviation for NOT
        APPLICABLE
43. Short for ABDOMEN
44. Steal
46. Leaf of a tea plant
47. Abbreviation for BROTHER
49. At
50. Give me _ _ apple.
51. Tardy
54. Cent
56. The Wizard of ____
58. Opposite of Father
60. Negative
61. Saying
62. Same as 57 DOWN

DOWN

1. A brass instrument
2. Abbreviation for aluminum
3. A legal document that says who
    gets what
4. Opposite of NEW
5. Currency
6. An exclamation
7. Latin, Spanish and Italian
    for FROM
8. Abbreviation for DOCTOR
9. Hitler's secret police
11. Having life
12. Work
15. Opposite of STOP
16. Important period of time
17. A part of a seam
19. Eleven in Rome
20. Years a person has lived
21. Same as 7 DOWN
22. White, rye, wheat, etc.
23. Second place in the Olympics
24. Opposite of ALWAYS
26. Very
29. Myself
30. Snatch away
31. Two in Rome
33. Famous singer who wears
    outrageous clothes
36. Abbreviation for CALIFORNIA
37. Opposite of LATE
38. Short for KANGAROO
40. Word in the Golden Rule
41. See
42. Number on a baseball team
46. Another word for FAUCET
48. Twelve
52. Hour of the day
55. Move the head
56. Exclamation of surprise
57. Negative prefix
59. Bye Bye: Ta __ __
60. Negative word

AB	NA
AC	NEVER
ADAGE	NINE
AE	NO
AGE	NOD
AL	NOR
ALL	NOT
AN	ODDS
AND	OH
BEST	OK
BR	OLD
BREAD	OTHERS
CA	OZ
CHEAPER	PENNY
CHER	REX
DE	ROB
DR	ROO
DOZEN	RULE
EARLY	SAYING
EE	SAX
EMIT	SI
ERA	SILVER
GO	STITCH
GOLD	SO
GOLDEN	SOIL
GRAB	SS
II	TA
IT	TAP
IV	TI
LATE	TIL
LIE	TIME
LIFE	TO
LOOK	TOIL
ME	UNTO
MONEY	WILL
MOTHER	WORM
	XI

ABBREVIATIONS

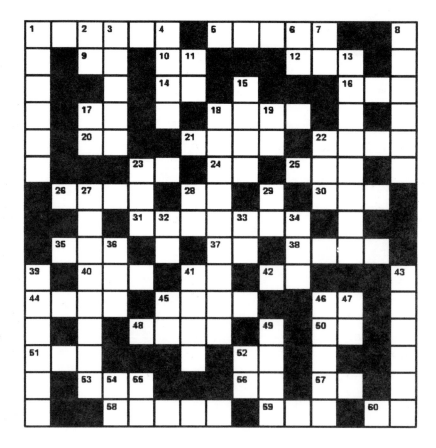

ACROSS

1. Prefix meaning around
5. Structure to keep animals in
9. Beginning of church
10. Abbreviation for EACH
12. Consumed
14. Toward
16. Nickname for Thomas
17. RAILROAD
18. Intend
20. ROAD: abbrev.
21. Geek
22. Celebration
23. Except after C
24. North Dakota
25. Drawing, painting
26. Crazy
28. Toward
30. First three vowels
31. Countries
35. Prefix meaning WITH or TOGETHER
37. Upon
38. Line of stitches
40. Abbreviation for MEDICINE
41. Within
42. Us
44. Abbreviation for QUESTION
45. Singles
46. Be quiet!
48. Mothers Against Drunk Driving
50. Two in Rome
51. Abbreviation for AVENUE
52. Abbreviation for EUROPEAN UNION
53. Male sheep
56. Leaf of a tea plant
57. Six in Latin
58. Intends
59. Finger on the foot
60. Northeast: abbreviation

DOWN

1. Round shape
2. Abbreviation for ROMAN
    CATHOLIC
3. Line across a circle
4. Flesh
6. Abbreviation for CALIFORNIA
7. AND in Rome
8. Amount
11. Toward
13. And so forth
15. Geek
17. Railroad
18. Said briefly in passing
19. Letters meaning years after Christ's
    birth
22. Title for a monk
23. A charged atom
27. Dial which records distance covered
28. Toward
29. On top of
32. Exist
33. Same as 29 DOWN
34. Abbreviation for a compass direction
37. Opposite of OFF
36. Prefix meaning a combination of parts
39. Shape having 4 right angles
41. Prefix meaning Combined with things
    East Indian
43. The number of Apostles in the
    Christian Bible
45. Middle of the BOAT
46. Strainer
47. Hello
49. Set of clothes
52. Same as 7 DOWN
54. Exist
55. Myself

AD	
AEI	MEANS
AM	MEAT
ART	MED
AT	MENTIONED
ATE	MES
AVE	ND
CA	NE
CH	NATIONS
CHORD	NERD
CIRCLE	NUMBER
CIRCUM	OA
COM	ODOMETER
EA	ON
ET	ONES
ET CETERA	QUES
EU	RAM
FENCE	RC
FETE	RD
FRA	RR
HI	SEAM
IE	SH
II	SIEVE
IN	SSE
INDO	SQUARE
ION	SUIT
LOCO	TI
MADD	TOE
ME	TOM
MEAN	TWELVE
	VI
	WE

ACE

ACROSS

1. Opposite of girl
3. Come nearer
9. A girl's name
10. Letter before S, phonetically
11. Toward
13. Japanese robe
15. Milliliter: abbrev
16. Hark! (In the Bible)
17. Put together
19. Less expensive
21. Spanish for GOLD
23. Very
24. See 11 ACROSS
25. 57 minus 55
26. Unite

27. First two letters of CHURCH
29. Unhappy
31. Busy as a _ _ _
32. Sound of Surprise
33. A doctor has this degree
34. Shaft of sunlight
38. "Come here" in Spanish
39. See 7 DOWN
40. Cut-off trousers
42. A little bit
43. Abbreviation for DOCTOR
45. Same as 40 DOWN
46. Soil
47. Speak

DOWN

2. Slang for HELLO
3. Having life
4. Nickname for Pamela
5. Professional: abbrev.
6. Went fast
7. Exist
8. Stop
11. In addition
12. Toward
14. Singular for OURSELVES
　　　(Bad grammar)
15. Mine in Italian
18. Partner of OR
19. One who works with cattle
20. Rhymes with SAM
22. Route: abbrev
24. Highest card in the deck
26. Put together
28. Halos
30. Same as 20 DOWN
31. Foods made from wheat
35. Letter before "ES"
36. Now I see!
37. Heavenly body
40. Station: abbrev.
41. Not even
44. Ancient Egyptian god

ACE
ADD
AHA
AIN
ALIVE
ALSO
AM
APPROACH
AR
AT
AURAS
BEE
BOY
BREADS
CH
CHEAPER
COWBOY
DIRT
DR
EITHER
HALT
KIMONO
LARA
LO
MD

MIA
ML
ODD
OH
ORO
OURSELF
PAM
PR
PRO
RA
RAN
RAY
RT
SAD
SAY
SHORTS
SO
STA
STAR
TAD
TO
TWO
UNITE
UP
VEN
YO

MISTER

ACROSS

1. Plaything
3. Mister in Mexico and Spain: abbrev.
4. Polite form of address
8. Leaf of a tea plant
9. Ancient Egyptian god
10. Elated
12. Three feet
14. Common Era (also A.D.)
15. Expert
16. Part of the personality
17. Old fashioned blackboard
20. Reach
21. Opposite of east
23. Age, period of time

24. Less expensive
28. One of the Three Stooges
30. Spanish of gold
32. Kind of antelope
33. What you do with oars
34. Short for UNTIL
35. Saying
38. Little _ _ Beep
40. So
42. Animal used for work and pleasure
45. Do, Re, _ _
46. Opposite of GIRL
47. Float gently

DOWN

1. Toward
2. Old fashioned YES
3. Eat, dine
4. Do, Re, _ _
5. Señora: abbrev.
6. Black goo for sealing things
7. Egyptian god
10. Aid
11. Ache
12. Day before today
13. A small spot
15. Consumed
18. First man in the Bible
19. Make easier, loosen
20. Mister in Mexico and Spain
22. Encounter
24. One who works with cattle
25. Having life
26. Without much color
27. Spanish for IN
29. Organization: abbrev.
31. OR backwards
36. Same as C.E.
37. Send; spew out
39. Partner of EITHER
41. Uncooked
42. Part of what Santa says
43. Very
44. Coming from

ACE	OF
AD	OR
ADAGE	ORG
ADAM	ORO
ALIVE	PAIN
ATE	PALE
BO	RA
BOY	RAW
CE	RO
CHEAPER	ROW
COWBOY	SEÑOR
DOT	SLATE
EASE	SO
ELAND	SPAN
EMIT	SRA
ERA	SUP
HAPPY	TAR
HELP	TI
HO	TI
HORSE	TO
ID	TOY
MAP	VERY
MEET	WAFT
MI	WEST
MISTER	YARD
MOE	YEA
MR	YESTERDAY

ANSWERS

page 9

page 11

page 13

page 15

-44-

page 17

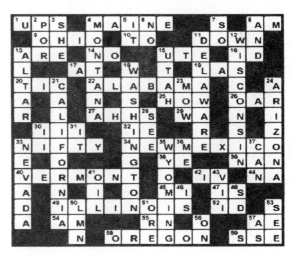

page 19

page 21

page 23

page 25

page 27

page 29

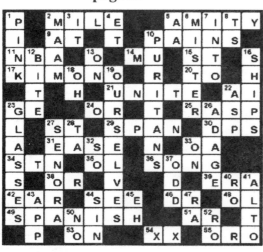

page 31

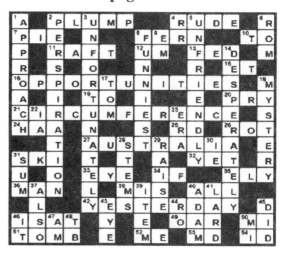

page 33

page 35

page 37

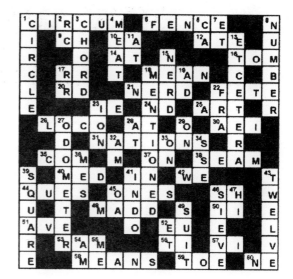

page 39

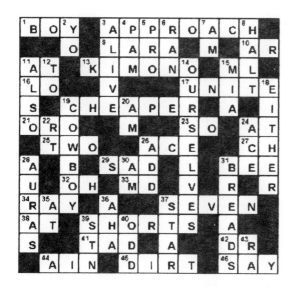

page 41

page 43

YOU DID IT!

NEW WORDS I'VE LEARNED